Mind Diet Cookbook for One

Boost Your Brain Health, Help Prevent Alzheimer's and Dementia with One Delicious Solo Meal at a Time

By

Dr. Tate Mandara

Table of Contents

INTRODUCTION.. 7

CHAPTER ONE.. 11

Understanding the Mind Diet........................11

Benefits of Adopting the Mind Diet.................12

Foods to Eat and Avoid.................................14

Tips for Successful Solo Cooking................... 18

CHAPTER TWO.. 21

Mind Diet and Cooking For One.....................21

Tailoring the Mind Diet to Individual
Needs..21

Essential Ingredients for a Mindful
Kitchen... 23

Smart Shopping for Single Servings......... 25

CHAPTER THREE... 29

Breakfast Recipes.......................................29

Nutty Oatmeal.. 29

Banana Cookies...................................... 30

Strawberry Yoghurt..................................32

Quinoa Porridge......................................33

Whole Grain Breakfast Porridge.............. 34

Chickpea Cookie Dough........................... 36

Berry Bliss Smoothie................................37

Bean Pate.. 38

Breakfast Croissant..................................39

CHAPTER FOUR.. **41**

Lunch Recipes... 41

Greek Chicken Pita Pocket....................... 41

Spicy Citrus Shrimp Salad........................ 42

Cheesy Turkey Pan....................................44

Portobello Sandwiches..............................46

Chili Collard Greens.................................. 47

Brussels Sprout Salad...............................49

Chicken Tacos...51

Mediterranean Tuna Salad........................52

CHAPTER FIVE...**55**

Dinner Recipes..55

Cumin Salmon...55

Vegetable Succotash................................ 56

Pesto Zoodles with Cherry Tomatoes....... 58

Chicken Couscous.................................... 59

Cashew Turkey Medley..............................60

Walnut-Crusted Baked Cod.......................62

Baked Mackerel.. 63

Colorful Gumbo...65

CHAPTER SIX..**67**

Soup & Stew Recipes.................................... 67

Moroccan Lentil Stew................................67

Spicy Tomato Basil Bisque........................69

Coconut Curry Chickpea Stew.................. 71

Broccoli and Cheddar Soup...................... 73

One-Pot Chicken Noodle Soup................. 75

Tuscan White Bean Stew..........................77

Butternut Squash Soup...........................79

Spinach and White Bean Soup.................81

CHAPTER SIX..**83**

Fish & Seafood..83

Herb-Crusted Cod Fillet.........................83

Sea Bass...85

Chives Trout..86

Citrus Baked Tilapia...............................88

Ginger Halibut...89

Tuna Puttanesca.....................................91

Miso Glazed Black Cod...........................93

Shrimp and Spinach Spaghetti................94

CHAPTER EIGHT.....................................**97**

Salad Recipes...97

Breakfast Salad.......................................97

Brain Healthy Salad................................98

Caprese Salad Skewers........................100

Superfood Quinoa Salad........................101

Asian-Inspired Sesame Ginger Salad.....102

Tabbouleh Salad....................................104

Mediterranean Chickpea Salad..............105

Classic Greek Salad..............................106

CHAPTER NINE....................................**109**

Snack Recipes.......................................109

Fried Mushrooms....................................109

Zucchini Dip.................................110
Cauliflower Popcorn..........................111
Almond Butter Stuffed Dates.................. 113
Rainbow Fruit Salad.......................... 114
Carrot Cashew Pâté........................... 115
Snacky Chickpeas.............................116
Bruschetta................................... 118
Edamame with Sea Salt........................ 119

CHAPTER TEN.................................. **121**
Dessert Recipes..............................121
Chickpea Blondies............................ 121
Homestyle Apple Pie..........................122
Cranberry Pear Crisp......................... 124
Summer Fruit Pops............................ 125
Banana Nut Mug Cake..........................126
Blueberry Tahini Crisp....................... 127
Greek Yogurt Berry Popsicles................. 128
Maple Pecan Granola with Olive Oil....... 129

7-DAY MEAL PLAN..............................**131**
Day 1.. 131
Day 2.. 131
Day 3.. 131
Day 4.. 132
Day 5.. 132
Day 6.. 132
Day 7.. 132
CONCLUSION...................................**135**

INTRODUCTION

Welcome to the "Mind Diet Cookbook For One," a culinary journey designed to enhance cognitive function and promote brain health. In an era where the significance of mental well-being is increasingly recognized, this cookbook serves as a practical guide for individuals looking to nourish their minds through mindful eating. As we age, the importance of maintaining cognitive vitality becomes paramount. This cookbook tailors its recipes for solo dining, recognizing the diverse needs of individuals, with a particular focus on the Mind Diet—an approach known for its positive impact on brain health. The Mind Diet emphasizes the consumption of nutrient-rich foods such as leafy greens, berries, nuts, and fish, which have been linked to cognitive benefits and a reduced risk of neurodegenerative diseases.

Silas Matt, a senior grappling with Alzheimer's and dementia, found solace and empowerment within the pages of this cookbook. By embracing the Mind Diet principles and adapting recipes to suit his solitary meals, Silas experienced notable improvements in cognitive function. This cookbook not only provided him with delicious and easy-to-prepare recipes but also offered valuable insights into managing neurodegenerative conditions. Silas's journey showcases the transformative potential of mindful eating, demonstrating how a well-crafted diet can contribute not only to physical health but also to the preservation of cognitive abilities. Moreover, Silas's story extends beyond personal health benefits. The cookbook's emphasis on single-serving recipes contributes to minimizing food waste, aligning with a sustainable and responsible approach to nutrition. "Mind Diet Cookbook For One" is not just a collection of recipes; it's a lifestyle guide that empowers individuals to take charge of their brain health while fostering a conscientious relationship with food.

CHAPTER ONE

Understanding the Mind Diet

The Mind Diet stands as a dietary approach meticulously crafted to nurture cognitive health and reduce the risk of neurodegenerative disorders. Rooted in scientific research, this regimen emphasizes the consumption of nutrient-dense foods recognized for their positive impact on the brain. Leafy greens, berries, nuts, fish, and olive oil take center stage in this dietary paradigm, providing a rich source of antioxidants, omega-3 fatty acids, and other essential nutrients.

By promoting a plant-centric and Mediterranean-inspired eating style, the Mind Diet not only fuels the body but also supports mental clarity and resilience. This approach underscores the importance of minimizing processed foods and embracing whole, natural ingredients. Studies have suggested that adhering to the Mind Diet may contribute to cognitive benefits, making it a promising avenue for those seeking to proactively nurture their brain health as they navigate the complexities of modern life. Understanding the Mind Diet unveils a holistic perspective on nutrition, intertwining the threads of mindful eating and cognitive well-being.

Benefits of Adopting the Mind Diet

Embracing the Mind Diet offers a myriad of benefits that extend beyond just physical health. Primarily designed to nourish the brain, this dietary approach has been associated with a reduced risk of cognitive decline and neurodegenerative disorders. Rich in fruits, vegetables, whole grains, nuts, and fish, the Mind Diet provides a wealth of nutrients, including antioxidants and omega-3 fatty acids, known for their positive impact on brain function.

One notable benefit is improved cognitive performance. Studies suggest that adhering to the Mind Diet may enhance memory, attention, and overall cognitive abilities. Additionally, this dietary pattern has been linked to a lower risk of developing conditions like Alzheimer's disease and dementia.

Beyond cognitive health, adopting the Mind Diet contributes to overall well-being. The emphasis on plant-based foods and healthy fats supports heart health, reduces inflammation, and aids in weight management.

The inclusion of nutrient-dense foods also fortifies the immune system, promoting resilience against various health challenges. Moreover, the Mind Diet promotes a sustainable and balanced relationship with food. With its focus on natural, unprocessed ingredients, this approach encourages individuals to make mindful and conscientious choices, fostering a positive impact on both personal health and the environment. In essence, the Mind Diet emerges as a holistic lifestyle choice, nurturing physical and mental well-being through the power of nutrient-rich, flavorful foods.

Foods to Eat and Avoid

The Mind Diet champions a nutrient-rich approach to nourishing the brain, emphasizing a diverse array of wholesome foods. Leafy greens, such as kale and spinach, take center stage, offering a wealth of vitamins, minerals, and antioxidants vital for cognitive health. Berries, particularly blueberries and strawberries, are celebrated for their potent flavonoids that may help combat oxidative stress.

Incorporating nuts, especially walnuts, and seeds like flaxseeds and chia seeds, provides a source of omega-3 fatty acids crucial for brain function. Whole grains, such as oats, quinoa, and brown rice, contribute complex carbohydrates and essential nutrients, promoting sustained energy.

Fatty fish, like salmon and trout, deliver omega-3s and lean protein, supporting cognitive well-being. Poultry and eggs are additional protein sources recommended in moderation. Olive oil, a staple in Mediterranean cuisine, serves as a healthy source of monounsaturated fats.

This diet encourages a plant-centric approach, emphasizing fruits, vegetables, and legumes. The Mind Diet is not just a collection of ingredients but a holistic lifestyle choice, harnessing the power of nature's bounty to promote cognitive vitality and overall well-being.

Foods to Avoid

The Mind Diet advocates for the exclusion or limited consumption of certain foods associated with potential cognitive decline and negative impacts on overall health. Red meat is advised to be limited, as its high saturated fat content may contribute to cardiovascular issues linked with impaired cognitive function. Similarly, butter and margarine, known for their unhealthy fats, are suggested to be minimized due to their potential adverse effects on heart health.

Processed sweets and pastries, high in refined sugars and unhealthy fats, are discouraged in the Mind Diet to mitigate the risk of inflammation and oxidative stress. Fried and fast foods, recognized for their detrimental impact on cardiovascular health, are also on the list of foods to avoid or consume sparingly.

By steering clear of these less nutritious options and adopting a diet rich in fruits, vegetables, whole grains, and lean proteins, individuals following the Mind Diet aim to cultivate not only a resilient and healthy brain but also support overall well-being. This dietary approach underscores the importance of making mindful and informed choices to positively influence cognitive function and reduce the risk of neurodegenerative diseases.

Tips for Successful Solo Cooking

Successful solo cooking is an art that combines efficiency, creativity, and enjoyment. Plan your meals to streamline the cooking process and minimize waste. Embrace versatile ingredients that can be used in multiple dishes, allowing for variety without excess. Invest in kitchen tools suitable for smaller portions, optimizing the cooking experience. Batch cooking and freezing portions can save time on busy days.

Experiment with spices and herbs to elevate flavors without complexity. Opt for simple, balanced recipes to avoid overwhelm. Utilize fresh produce and explore local markets for seasonal inspiration. Maintain a well-organized kitchen to enhance efficiency and ease.

Enjoy the process—solo cooking can be a therapeutic and rewarding experience. Adjust recipes to suit personal tastes and dietary preferences. By incorporating these tips, solo cooking transforms from a routine task into a fulfilling and enjoyable culinary adventure.

CHAPTER TWO

Mind Diet and Cooking For One

Tailoring the Mind Diet to Individual Needs

Tailoring the Mind Diet to individual needs involves a personalized approach to optimizing brain health. While the Mind Diet provides a robust framework, flexibility is crucial to accommodate various preferences and dietary requirements. Individuals can adapt the diet based on factors like age, activity level, and specific health goals.

For those with dietary restrictions or preferences, substitutions can be made while staying true to the diet's core principles.

Vegetarians, for example, can rely on plant-based sources of omega-3 fatty acids, such as flaxseeds and chia seeds, while still enjoying the benefits of these essential nutrients.

Considering cultural influences and culinary preferences is integral to adherence. Incorporating familiar flavors and dishes helps individuals sustain the Mind Diet in the long term. Regional variations can be integrated, ensuring that the diet remains accessible and enjoyable. Portion control is another aspect of personalization. Adapting the Mind Diet to individual energy needs prevents overconsumption and aligns with weight management goals.

Furthermore, individuals can experiment with meal timing and frequency based on personal schedules and preferences, as long as they maintain the overall nutrient balance advocated by the diet. In essence, tailoring the Mind Diet recognizes the uniqueness of each individual's journey toward better brain health. By embracing adaptability and making informed choices, individuals can create a sustainable and effective version of the Mind Diet that resonates with their lifestyle, ensuring both cognitive benefits and personal satisfaction.

Essential Ingredients for a Mindful Kitchen

Crafting a mindful kitchen aligned with the principles of the Mind Diet involves curating essential ingredients that nourish both the body and the brain. At the core of this mindful approach is an emphasis on whole, unprocessed foods. Leafy greens, such as kale and spinach, form a nutritional powerhouse, rich in vitamins and antioxidants crucial for cognitive health.

Incorporating an array of colorful berries, like blueberries and strawberries, introduces potent antioxidants, combating oxidative stress and supporting brain function. Essential fatty acids, abundant in nuts and seeds, contribute to cognitive well-being, offering a wholesome source of omega-3s.

Whole grains, a cornerstone of the Mind Diet, provide sustained energy and essential nutrients. Olive oil, a staple in Mediterranean cuisine, not only adds flavor but also delivers heart-healthy monounsaturated fats. Fatty fish, such as salmon and trout, supply omega-3 fatty acids vital for brain health.

Herbs and spices like turmeric, known for its anti-inflammatory properties, add both flavor and potential cognitive benefits.

Poultry and lean proteins contribute to a balanced diet, supporting overall health. Minimizing processed sugars and unhealthy fats is integral to a mindful kitchen. Choosing local, seasonal produce not only ensures freshness but also aligns with sustainable practices.

By stocking a mindful kitchen with these essential ingredients, individuals can seamlessly integrate the Mind Diet into their daily lives, fostering not just nutritional well-being but also a deeper connection with the food they consume.

Smart Shopping for Single Servings

Smart shopping for single servings, aligned with the Mind Diet principles, involves strategic choices to optimize nutrition and minimize waste.

Begin by planning meals, crafting a concise shopping list that caters specifically to individual needs. Prioritize fresh produce, selecting a variety of colorful fruits and vegetables, as these form the foundation of the Mind Diet and offer a spectrum of essential nutrients.

When it comes to protein, opt for smaller portions of lean meats, poultry, or fish, considering both nutritional requirements and minimizing potential leftovers. Utilize the versatility of canned beans and legumes, which provide plant-based protein and can be portioned for solo meals. Incorporate whole grains like quinoa or brown rice, which are available in single-serving options and offer a wholesome base for diverse recipes.

Explore the local market for seasonal ingredients, not only ensuring freshness but also supporting sustainable practices. Embrace frozen fruits and vegetables, which retain their nutritional value and can be used in smaller quantities, reducing the risk of spoilage. Mindful shopping involves reading labels to avoid processed foods and opting for products with minimal additives.

Investing in reusable containers can facilitate portion control and assist in storing perishables effectively, minimizing food waste. Consider joining a bulk foods section to purchase grains, nuts, and seeds in the desired quantities, reducing packaging and cost. In essence, smart shopping for single servings related to the Mind Diet involves a thoughtful and intentional approach, ensuring that each item selected contributes to a balanced, nutritious, and waste-conscious culinary experience.

CHAPTER THREE

Breakfast Recipes

Nutty Oatmeal

Serving: One

Cooking Time: 10 minutes

Ingredients:

•1/2 cup rolled oats

•1 cup unsweetened almond milk

•1 tablespoon nut butter

•1/4 cup mixed nuts (almonds, walnuts, or pecans)

•1/2 teaspoon cinnamon

Preparation:

1. In a saucepan, bring the almond milk to a simmer.

2. Stir in the rolled oats and cook for 5-7 minutes until creamy.

3. Mix in the nut butter, mixed nuts, and cinnamon.

4. Transfer to a bowl and serve hot.

Nutritional value (approximate): 400 calories, 12g protein, 8g fiber, 20g fat, 45g carbohydrates

Banana Cookies

Serving: One
Cooking Time: 20 minutes

Ingredients:

•1 ripe banana, mashed

•1/2 cup oats

•2 tablespoons nut butter

•1/4 teaspoon cinnamon

•1/4 teaspoon vanilla extract

Preparation:

1. Preheat the oven to 350°F (175°C) and line a baking sheet with parchment paper.

2. In a bowl, mix the mashed banana, oats, nut butter, cinnamon, and vanilla extract.

3. Drop spoonfuls of the mixture onto the baking sheet and flatten into cookie shapes.

4. Bake for 15 minutes until golden brown. Let cool before serving.

Nutritional value (approximate): 300 calories, 7g protein, 6g fiber, 12g fat, 40g carbohydrates

Strawberry Yoghurt

Serving: One

Preparation Time: 5 minutes

Ingredients:

- 1 cup Greek yogurt
- 1/2 cup fresh strawberries, sliced
- 1 tablespoon honey or maple syrup
- 1 tablespoon chia seeds

Preparation:

1. In a bowl, layer the Greek yogurt, sliced strawberries, and chia seeds.

2. Drizzle with honey or maple syrup. Serve immediately.

Nutritional value (approximate): 250 calories, 20g protein, 5g fiber, 8g fat, 25g carbohydrates

Quinoa Porridge

Serving: One
Cooking Time: 15 minutes

Ingredients:

•1/2 cup quinoa

•1 cup unsweetened almond milk

•1/2 teaspoon cinnamon

•1/4 cup mixed berries

•1 tablespoon honey or maple syrup

Preparation:

1. Rinse the quinoa under cold water.

2. In a saucepan, combine the quinoa and almond milk. Bring to a boil, then reduce the heat and simmer for 12-15 minutes, or until the quinoa is cooked and the mixture has thickened.

3. Stir in the cinnamon and honey or maple syrup.

4. Transfer to a bowl, top with mixed berries, and serve hot.

Nutritional value (approximate): 350 calories, 10g protein, 6g fiber, 8g fat, 55g carbohydrates

Whole Grain Breakfast Porridge

Serving: One
Cooking Time: 15 minutes

Ingredients:
•1/2 cup whole grain cereal (such as steel-cut oats or quinoa)
•1 cup unsweetened almond milk
•1/2 apple, chopped

•1/4 cup chopped nuts (such as almonds or walnuts)

•1/2 teaspoon cinnamon

Preparation:

1. In a saucepan, bring the almond milk to a simmer.

2. Stir in the whole grain cereal and cook for 10-12 minutes until tender.

3. Mix in the chopped apple, chopped nuts, and cinnamon.

4. Transfer to a bowl and serve hot.

Nutritional value (approximate): 400 calories, 12g protein, 8g fiber, 20g fat, 45g carbohydrates

Chickpea Cookie Dough

Serving: One

Cooking Time: 5 minutes

Ingredients:

•1/2 cup canned chickpeas, drained and rinsed

•2 tablespoons nut butter

•1 tablespoon honey or maple syrup

•1/4 teaspoon vanilla extract

•Pinch of salt

•1/4 cup dark chocolate chips

Preparation:

1. In a food processor, blend the chickpeas, nut butter, honey or maple syrup, vanilla extract, and salt until smooth.

2. Stir in the dark chocolate chips.

3. Transfer to a bowl and serve.

Nutritional value (approximate): 400 calories, 12g protein, 8g fiber, 20g fat, 45g carbohydrates

Berry Bliss Smoothie

Serving: One
Cooking Time: 5 minutes

Ingredients:
•1/2 cup frozen mixed berries
•1/2 banana
•1/2 cup unsweetened almond milk
•1/2 cup Greek yogurt
•1 tablespoon honey or maple syrup

Preparation:

1. Combine all ingredients in a blender and blend until smooth.

2. Pour into a glass and serve.

Nutritional value (approximate): 250 calories, 15g protein, 5g fiber, 5g fat, 40g carbohydrates

Bean Pate

Serving: One

Cooking Time: 10 minutes

Ingredients:

•1/2 cup canned white beans, drained and rinsed

•1/4 cup chopped nuts (such as almonds or walnuts)

•1 tablespoon olive oil

•1/2 teaspoon garlic powder

•Salt and pepper, to taste

Preparation:

1. In a food processor, blend the white beans, chopped nuts, olive oil, garlic powder, salt, and pepper until smooth.

2. Transfer to a bowl and serve with whole grain crackers or sliced vegetables.

Nutritional value (approximate): 300 calories, 10g protein, 6g fiber, 15g fat, 30g carbohydrates

Breakfast Croissant

Serving: One
Cooking Time: 10 minutes

Ingredients:
•1 croissant

•1 egg

•1 slice of cheese

•1 slice of turkey or ham

•Salt and pepper, to taste

Preparation:

1. Preheat the oven to 350°F (175°C).

2. Slice the croissant in half and place the bottom half on a baking sheet.

3. Layer the cheese and turkey or ham on top of the croissant.

4. Crack the egg into a small bowl and whisk with salt and pepper.

5. Pour the egg over the turkey or ham. Place the top half of the croissant on top of the egg.

6. Bake for 8-10 minutes until the egg is cooked and the cheese is melted. Serve hot.

CHAPTER FOUR

Lunch Recipes

Greek Chicken Pita Pocket

Serving: One
Cooking Time: 20 minutes

Ingredients:
- 3 oz grilled chicken breast, sliced
- 1 small whole-wheat pita
- 1/4 cup diced tomatoes
- 1/4 cup diced cucumbers
- 2 tbsp plain Greek yogurt
- 1/2 tbsp fresh lemon juice
- 1/2 tsp dried oregano

Preparation:

1. In a small bowl, mix the Greek yogurt, lemon juice, and dried oregano to make the dressing.

2. Warm the whole wheat pita in a toaster or oven.

3. Stuff the pita with the grilled chicken, tomatoes, and cucumbers.

4. Drizzle the Greek yogurt dressing over the filling. Serve immediately.

Nutritional value (approximate): 350 calories, 30g protein, 6g fiber, 8g fat, 35g carbohydrates

Spicy Citrus Shrimp Salad

Serving: One

Cooking Time: 15 minutes

Ingredients:

•4 oz cooked shrimp

•2 cups mixed greens (spinach, arugula, or kale)

•1/2 orange, segmented

•1/4 cup sliced red onions

•1/4 avocado, sliced

•1/2 tbsp olive oil

•1/2 tbsp fresh lime juice

•1/4 tsp chili powder

Preparation:

1. In a small bowl, whisk together the olive oil, lime juice, and chili powder to make the dressing.

2. Arrange the mixed greens in a large bowl or plate.

3. Top with the cooked shrimp, orange segments, red onions, and avocado.

4. Drizzle the dressing over the salad.

5. Toss gently to combine. Serve immediately.

Nutritional value (approximate): 300 calories, 25g protein, 8g fiber, 12g fat, 20g carbohydrates

Cheesy Turkey Pan

Serving: One
Cooking Time: 25 minutes

Ingredients:
•3 oz ground turkey
•1/2 cup cooked quinoa
•1/4 cup diced bell peppers
•1/4 cup diced onions
•1/4 cup shredded low-fat mozzarella cheese

•1/2 tsp olive oil

•1/2 tsp Italian seasoning

Preparation:

1. In a non-stick skillet, heat the olive oil over medium heat.

2. Add the ground turkey, bell peppers, and onions. Cook until the turkey is browned and the vegetables are tender.

3. Stir in the cooked quinoa and Italian seasoning. Cook for an additional 2-3 minutes.

4. Sprinkle the shredded mozzarella cheese on top and cover the skillet until the cheese is melted.

5. Transfer to a plate and serve hot.

Nutritional value (approximate): 400 calories, 35g protein, 5g fiber, 15g fat, 30g carbohydrates

Portobello Sandwiches

Serving: One
Cooking Time: 30 minutes

Ingredients:

•2 large portobello mushroom caps

•1/4 cup sliced red bell peppers

•1/4 cup sliced zucchini

•2 tbsp balsamic vinegar

•1 garlic clove, minced

•1/2 tbsp olive oil

•2 slices whole grain bread

Preparation:

1. Preheat the oven to 400°F (200°C).

2. In a small bowl, whisk together the balsamic vinegar, minced garlic, and olive oil.

3. Brush the portobello mushroom caps, red bell peppers, and zucchini with the balsamic mixture.

4. Roast the vegetables in the oven for 20 minutes, or until tender.

5. Assemble the portobello sandwiches with the roasted vegetables between the whole grain bread slices. Serve immediately.

Nutritional value (approximate): 320 calories, 12g protein, 8g fiber, 10g fat, 45g carbohydrates

Chili Collard Greens

Serving: One

Cooking Time: 30 minutes

Ingredients:

•1/2 lb ground turkey

•1/2 onion, chopped

•1/2 red bell pepper, chopped

•1 garlic clove, minced

•1/2 tsp chili powder

•1/2 tsp cumin

•1/2 tsp paprika

•1/2 cup canned diced tomatoes

•1/2 cup canned black beans, drained and rinsed

•2 large collard green leaves

Preparation:

1. In a large skillet, cook the ground turkey over medium heat until browned.

2. Add the onion, red bell pepper, and garlic. Cook until the vegetables are tender.

3. Stir in the chili powder, cumin, and paprika. Add the canned diced tomatoes and black beans. Simmer for 10-15 minutes.

4. Meanwhile, remove the stems from the collard green leaves and blanch them in boiling water for 1-2 minutes.

5. Place the collard green leaves on a plate and spoon the chili on top. Serve hot.

Nutritional value (approximate): 400 calories, 30g protein, 12g fiber, 15g fat, 40g carbohydrates

Brussels Sprout Salad

Serving: One

Cooking Time: 20 minutes

Ingredients:

•1 cup Brussels sprouts, trimmed and halved

•1/4 cup chopped walnuts

•1/4 cup dried cranberries

•1/4 cup crumbled feta cheese

•1/2 tbsp olive oil

•1/2 tbsp balsamic vinegar

•Salt and pepper, to taste

Preparation:

1. Preheat the oven to 400°F (200°C).

2. Toss the Brussels sprouts with olive oil, salt, and pepper.

3. Roast the Brussels sprouts in the oven for 15-20 minutes, or until tender and browned.

4. In a bowl, mix the roasted Brussels sprouts, chopped walnuts, dried cranberries,

crumbled feta cheese, balsamic vinegar, salt, and pepper. Serve immediately.

Nutritional value (approximate): 350 calories, 10g protein, 8g fiber, 20g fat, 30g carbohydrates

Chicken Tacos

Serving: One
Cooking Time: 20 minutes

Ingredients:

•3 oz cooked chicken breast, shredded

•2 small corn tortillas

•1/4 cup diced tomatoes

•1/4 cup diced onions

•1/4 avocado, sliced

•1/2 tbsp olive oil

•1/2 tbsp fresh lime juice

•1/4 tsp chili powder

Preparation:

1. Warm the corn tortillas in a toaster or oven.

2. In a small bowl, whisk together the olive oil, lime juice, and chili powder to make the dressing.
3. Stuff the tortillas with the shredded chicken, diced tomatoes, diced onions, and sliced avocado.

4. Drizzle the dressing over the filling. Serve immediately.

Nutritional value (approximate): 350 calories, 20g protein, 6g fiber, 12g fat, 40g carbohydrates

Mediterranean Tuna Salad

Serving: One
Cooking Time: 10 minutes

Ingredients:

•3 oz canned tuna, drained

•2 cups mixed greens (spinach, arugula, or kale)

•1/4 cup diced cucumbers

•1/4 cup diced tomatoes

•1/4 cup sliced Kalamata olives

•1/2 tbsp olive oil

•1/2 tbsp fresh lemon juice

•1/4 tsp dried oregano

Preparation:

1. In a small bowl, whisk together the olive oil, lemon juice, and dried oregano to make the dressing.

2. Arrange the mixed greens in a large bowl or plate.

3. Top with the canned tuna, diced cucumbers, diced tomatoes, and sliced Kalamata olives.

4. Drizzle the dressing over the salad.

5. Toss gently to combine. Serve immediately.

Nutritional value (approximate): 300 calories, 25g protein, 8g fiber, 12g fat, 20g carbohydrates

CHAPTER FIVE

Dinner Recipes

Cumin Salmon

Serving: One

Cooking Time: 15 minutes

Ingredients:

- 1 salmon fillet (4-6 oz)
- 1/2 tsp ground cumin
- 1/2 tsp olive oil
- Salt and pepper, to taste

Preparation:

1. Preheat the oven to 400°F (200°C).

2. Rub the salmon fillet with olive oil and sprinkle with ground cumin, salt, and pepper.

3. Place the salmon on a baking sheet and bake for 12-15 minutes, or until the salmon is cooked through. Serve hot.

Nutritional value (approximate): 300 calories, 25g protein, 0g fiber, 15g fat, 0g carbohydrates

Vegetable Succotash

Serving: One
Cooking Time: 20 minutes

Ingredients:
- 1/2 cup cooked lima beans
- 1/2 cup corn kernels
- 1/4 cup diced red bell pepper
- 1/4 cup diced onion
- 1/2 tbsp olive oil
- 1/2 tbsp fresh lemon juice
- 1/4 tsp dried thyme

Preparation:

1. In a skillet, heat the olive oil over medium heat.

2. Add the corn, red bell pepper, and onion.

3. Cook until the vegetables are tender.

4. Stir in the lima beans, dried thyme, and fresh lemon juice.

5. Cook for an additional 2-3 minutes. Serve hot.

Nutritional value (approximate): 250 calories, 10g protein, 8g fiber, 8g fat, 40g carbohydrates

Pesto Zoodles with Cherry Tomatoes

Serving: One
Cooking Time: 15 minutes

Ingredients:

•2 medium zucchinis, spiralized

•1/2 cup cherry tomatoes, halved

•2 tbsp basil pesto

•1/2 tbsp olive oil

•1/4 cup grated Parmesan cheese

Preparation:

1. In a skillet, heat the olive oil over medium heat.

2. Add the spiralized zucchini and cherry tomatoes. Cook for 3-5 minutes until the zucchini is tender.

3. Stir in the basil pesto and cook for an additional 1-2 minutes.

4. Transfer to a plate and sprinkle with grated Parmesan cheese. Serve hot.

Nutritional value (approximate): 200 calories, 8g protein, 6g fiber, 12g fat, 20g carbohydrates

Chicken Couscous

Serving: One
Cooking Time: 25 minutes

Ingredients:
•3 oz cooked chicken breast, diced
•1/2 cup cooked whole wheat couscous
•1/4 cup diced cucumbers
•1/4 cup diced tomatoes
•1/2 tbsp olive oil
•1/2 tbsp fresh lemon juice

•1/4 tsp dried oregano

Preparation:

1. In a bowl, mix the cooked chicken, whole wheat couscous, cucumbers, and tomatoes.

2. In a small bowl, whisk together the olive oil, lemon juice, and dried oregano to make the dressing.

3. Drizzle the dressing over the chicken couscous mixture. Serve hot or cold.

Nutritional value (approximate): 350 calories, 25g protein, 6g fiber, 10g fat, 40g carbohydrates

Cashew Turkey Medley

Serving: One
Cooking Time: 25 minutes

Ingredients:

•3 oz ground turkey

•1/4 cup cashews

•1/2 cup mixed vegetables (bell peppers, snap peas, carrots)

•1/2 tbsp olive oil

•1/2 tsp low-sodium soy sauce

Preparation:

1. In a skillet, heat the olive oil over medium heat.

2. Add the ground turkey and cook until browned.

3. Add the mixed vegetables and cashews.
4. Cook until the vegetables are tender.

5. Stir in the low-sodium soy sauce. Serve hot.

Nutritional value (approximate): 350 calories, 25g protein, 6g fiber, 15g fat, 30g carbohydrates

Walnut-Crusted Baked Cod

Serving: One

Cooking Time: 20 minutes

Ingredients:

•1 cod fillet (4-6 oz)

•2 tbsp crushed walnuts

•1/2 tbsp Dijon mustard

•1/2 tbsp olive oil

Preparation:

1. Preheat the oven to 400°F (200°C).

2. In a small bowl, mix the crushed walnuts and Dijon mustard.

3. Place the cod fillet on a baking sheet and brush with olive oil.

4. Spread the walnut mixture over the top of the cod filet.

5. Bake for 15-20 minutes, or until the cod is cooked through and the walnut crust is golden. Serve hot.

Nutritional value (approximate): 250 calories, 25g protein, 2g fiber, 12g fat, 5g carbohydrates

Baked Mackerel

Serving: One
Cooking Time: 25 minutes

Ingredients:
- 1 mackerel filet
- 1/2 lemon, sliced
- 1/2 tbsp olive oil
- 1/4 tsp dried dill

Preparation:

1. Preheat the oven to 375°F (190°C).

2. Place the mackerel fillet on a baking sheet.

3. Drizzle with olive oil and sprinkle with dried dill.

4. Arrange the lemon slices on top of the mackerel.

5. Bake for 20-25 minutes, or until the mackerel is cooked through. Serve hot.

Nutritional value (approximate): 300 calories, 20g protein, 0g fiber, 15g fat, 0g carbohydrates

Colorful Gumbo

Serving: One

Cooking Time: 40 minutes

Ingredients:

•3 oz cooked chicken breast, shredded

•1/2 cup okra, sliced

•1/4 cup bell peppers, diced

•1/4 cup onions, diced

•1/4 cup celery, diced

•1/2 cup cooked brown rice

•1/2 tbsp olive oil

•1/2 tbsp Cajun seasoning

Preparation:

1. In a large pot, heat the olive oil over medium heat.

2. Add the okra, bell peppers, onions, and celery. Cook until the vegetables are tender.

3. Stir in the shredded chicken and Cajun seasoning. Cook for an additional 5-7 minutes.

4. Serve the gumbo over the cooked brown rice.

Nutritional value (approximate): 400 calories, 30g protein, 8g fiber, 10g fat, 45g carbohydrates

CHAPTER SIX

Soup & Stew Recipes

Moroccan Lentil Stew

Serving: One
Cooking Time: 30 minutes

Ingredients:
- 1/2 cup brown lentils
- 1/2 cup chopped carrots
- 1/2 cup chopped celery
- 1/2 cup chopped onions
- 1/2 cup chopped tomatoes
- 1/2 cup chopped bell peppers
- 1/2 cup chopped zucchini
- 1/2 cup chopped spinach
- 1/2 tbsp olive oil
- 1/2 tbsp ground cumin
- 1/2 tbsp ground coriander

•Salt and pepper, to taste

Preparation:

1. In a large pot, heat the olive oil over medium heat.

2. Add the carrots, celery, onions, tomatoes, bell peppers, and zucchini. Cook until the vegetables are tender.

3. Stir in the spinach, ground cumin, and ground coriander. Cook for an additional 5 minutes.

4. Add the brown lentils and enough water to cover the lentils by 2 inches. Once the lentils are soft, reduce the heat and simmer for 20 to 25 minutes after bringing to a boil.

5. Season with salt and pepper to taste. Serve hot.

Nutritional value (approximate): 400 calories, 25g protein, 8g fiber, 15g fat, 40g carbohydrates

Spicy Tomato Basil Bisque

Serving: One
Cooking Time: 20 minutes

Ingredients:
- 1/2 cup diced tomatoes
- 1/2 cup chopped onions
- 1/2 cup chopped bell peppers
- 1/2 cup chopped zucchini
- 1/2 cup chopped carrots
- 1/2 cup chopped celery
- 1/2 tbsp olive oil
- 1/2 tbsp fresh lemon juice
- 1/4 tsp crushed red pepper flakes
- Salt and pepper, to taste

Preparation:

1. In a blender, combine the diced tomatoes, onions, bell peppers, zucchini, carrots, and celery. Blend until smooth.

2. In a large pot, heat the olive oil over medium heat.

3. Pour the tomato mixture into the pot and bring to a boil. Reduce the heat and simmer for 15-20 minutes, stirring occasionally, until slightly thickened.

4. Stir in the lemon juice, crushed red pepper flakes, salt, and pepper. Serve hot.

Nutritional value (approximate): 300 calories, 15g protein, 5g fiber, 10g fat, 20g carbohydrates

Coconut Curry Chickpea Stew

Serving: One
Cooking Time: 25 minutes

Ingredients:

•1/2 cup chopped onions

•1/2 cup chopped bell peppers

•1/2 cup chopped zucchini

•1/2 cup chopped carrots

•1/2 cup chopped celery

•1/2 tbsp olive oil

•1/2 tbsp curry powder

•1/2 cup canned chickpeas, drained and rinsed

•1/2 cup canned coconut milk

•Salt and pepper, to taste

Preparation:

1. In a large pot, heat the olive oil over medium heat.

2. Add the onions, bell peppers, zucchini, carrots, and celery. Cook until the vegetables are tender.

3. Stir in the curry powder and cook for an additional 1-2 minutes.

4. Add the chickpeas, coconut milk, and enough water to cover the ingredients by 2 inches.

5. Bring to a boil, then reduce the heat and simmer for 15-20 minutes, or until the stew is heated through.

6. Season with salt and pepper to taste. Serve hot.

Nutritional value (approximate): 400 calories, 25g protein, 8g fiber, 15g fat, 40g carbohydrates

Broccoli and Cheddar Soup

Serving one: 1
Cooking Time: 20 minutes

Ingredients:

•1/2 cup chopped onions

•1/2 cup chopped carrots

•1/2 cup chopped celery

•1/2 cup chopped broccoli

•1/2 cup shredded cheddar cheese

•1/2 tbsp olive oil

•1/2 tbsp all-purpose flour

•2 cups low-sodium vegetable broth

•Salt and pepper, to taste

Preparation:

1. In a large pot, heat the olive oil over medium heat.

2. Add the onions, carrots, celery, and broccoli. Cook until the vegetables are tender.

3. Stir in the flour and cook for an additional 1-2 minutes.

4. Slowly whisk in the vegetable broth and bring the soup to a boil. Reduce the heat and simmer for 10 minutes.

5. Stir in the shredded cheddar cheese and cook until the cheese is melted and the soup is heated through.

6. Season with salt and pepper to taste. Serve hot.

Nutritional value (approximate): 300 calories, 20g protein, 5g fiber, 10g fat, 30g carbohydrates

One-Pot Chicken Noodle Soup

Serving: One

Cooking Time: 30 minutes

Ingredients:

•3 oz cooked chicken breast, shredded

•1/2 cup chopped carrots

•1/2 cup chopped celery

•1/2 cup chopped onions

•1/2 cup whole grain egg noodles

•2 cups low-sodium chicken broth

•1/2 tbsp olive oil

•1/2 tbsp fresh parsley, chopped

•Salt and pepper, to taste

Preparation:

1. In a large pot, heat the olive oil over medium heat.

2. Add the carrots, celery, and onions. Cook until the vegetables are tender.

3. Pour in the chicken broth and bring to a boil.

4. Add the whole grain egg noodles and cook for 8-10 minutes, or until the noodles are all dente.

5. Stir in the shredded chicken and fresh parsley. Cook until the chicken is heated through.

6. Season with salt and pepper to taste. Serve hot.

Nutritional value (approximate): 350 calories, 25g protein, 5g fiber, 10g fat, 30g carbohydrates

Tuscan White Bean Stew

Serving: One

Cooking Time: 25 minutes

Ingredients:

•1/2 cup canned white beans, drained and rinsed

•1/2 cup chopped tomatoes

•1/2 cup chopped onions

•1/2 cup chopped carrots

•1/2 cup chopped celery

•1/2 cup low-sodium vegetable broth

•1/2 tbsp olive oil

•1/2 tsp dried rosemary

•Salt and pepper, to taste

Preparation:

1. In a large pot, heat the olive oil over medium heat.

2. Add the onions, carrots, and celery. Cook until the vegetables are tender.

3. Stir in the chopped tomatoes and dried rosemary. Cook for an additional 2-3 minutes.

4. Add the white beans and vegetable broth.

5. Bring to a boil, then reduce the heat and simmer for 15-20 minutes.

6. Season with salt and pepper to taste. Serve hot.

Nutritional value (approximate): 300 calories, 15g protein, 8g fiber, 10g fat, 35g carbohydrates

Butternut Squash Soup

Serving: One

Cooking Time: 30 minutes

Ingredients:

•1 cup butternut squash, peeled and cubed

•1/2 cup chopped onions

•1/2 cup chopped carrots

•1/2 cup low-sodium vegetable broth

•1/2 cup unsweetened almond milk

•1/2 tbsp olive oil

•1/4 tsp ground nutmeg

•Salt and pepper, to taste

Preparation:

1. In a large pot, heat the olive oil over medium heat.

2. Add the onions and carrots. Cook until the vegetables are tender.

3. Stir in the butternut squash, vegetable broth, and ground nutmeg. Bring to a boil, then reduce the heat and simmer for 15-20 minutes, or until the butternut squash is tender.

3. Use an immersion blender to puree the soup until smooth.

4. Stir in the unsweetened almond milk and cook for an additional 2-3 minutes.

5. Season with salt and pepper to taste. Serve hot.

Nutritional value (approximate): 250 calories, 5g protein, 8g fiber, 10g fat, 35g carbohydrates

Spinach and White Bean Soup

Serving: One
Cooking Time: 25 minutes

Ingredients:

• 1/2 cup canned white beans, drained and rinsed
• 1/2 cup chopped tomatoes
• 1/2 cup chopped onions
• 1/2 cup chopped carrots
• 1/2 cup chopped celery
• 1 cup chopped spinach
• 1/2 cup low-sodium vegetable broth
• 1/2 tbsp olive oil
• 1/2 tsp dried thyme
• Salt and pepper, to taste

Preparation:

1. In a large pot, heat the olive oil over medium heat.

2. Add the onions, carrots, and celery. Cook until the vegetables are tender.

3. Stir in the chopped tomatoes and dried thyme. Cook for an additional 2-3 minutes.

4. Add the white beans and vegetable broth.

5. Bring to a boil, then reduce the heat and simmer for 15-20 minutes.

6. Stir in the chopped spinach and cook until the spinach is wilted.

7. Season with salt and pepper to taste. Serve hot.

Nutritional value (approximate): 300 calories, 15g protein, 8g fiber, 10g fat, 35g carbohydrates

CHAPTER SIX

Fish & Seafood

Herb-Crusted Cod Fillet

Serving: One

Cooking Time: 20 minutes

Ingredients:

- 1/2 lb cod fillet
- 1/2 tbsp olive oil
- 1/2 tbsp chopped fresh parsley
- 1/2 tbsp chopped fresh basil
- 1/2 tbsp chopped fresh chives
- Salt and pepper, to taste

Preparation:

1. Preheat the oven to 400°F (204°C).

2. In a small bowl, mix the chopped parsley, basil, and chives.

3. Place the cod filet on a piece of parchment paper and drizzle with olive oil.

4. Sprinkle the herb mixture on top of the cod filet and pat it to adhere.

5. Place the cod filet on a baking sheet and bake in the preheated oven for 10-12 minutes, or until the cod flakes easily with a fork and is opaque in the center. Serve hot.

Nutritional value (approximate): 250 calories, 15g protein, 1g fiber, 10g fat, 8g carbohydrates

Sea Bass

Serving: One

Cooking Time: 20 minutes

Ingredients:

•1/2 lb sea bass filet

•1/2 tbsp olive oil

•Salt and pepper, to taste

Preparation:

1. Preheat the oven to 400°F (204°C).

2. In a small bowl, mix salt and pepper to taste.

3. Place the sea bass fillet on a piece of parchment paper and drizzle with olive oil.

4. Sprinkle the seasoning mixture on top of the sea bass filet and pat it to adhere.

5. Place the sea bass filet on a baking sheet and bake in the preheated oven for 10-12 minutes, or until the fish flakes easily with a fork and is opaque in the center. Serve hot.

Nutritional value (approximate): 250 calories, 15g protein, 1g fiber, 10g fat, 8g carbohydrates

Chives Trout

Serving: One
Cooking Time: 20 minutes

Ingredients:
•1/2 lb trout filet
•1/2 tbsp olive oil
•1/2 tbsp chopped fresh chives
•Salt and pepper, to taste

Preparation:

1. Preheat the oven to 400°F (204°C).

2. In a small bowl, mix chopped chives, salt, and pepper to taste.

3. Place the trout filet on a piece of parchment paper and drizzle with olive oil.

4. Sprinkle the chives mixture on top of the trout filet and pat it to adhere.

5. Place the trout filet on a baking sheet and bake in the preheated oven for 10-12 minutes, or until the fish flakes easily with a fork and is opaque in the center. Serve hot.

Nutritional value (approximate): 250 calories, 15g protein, 1g fiber, 10g fat, 8g carbohydrates

Citrus Baked Tilapia

Serving: One

Cooking Time: 20 minutes

Ingredients:

- 1/2 lb tilapia filet
- 1/2 tbsp olive oil
- 1/4 cup fresh orange juice
- 1/4 cup fresh lemon juice
- 1/4 cup fresh lime juice
- 1/2 tbsp chopped fresh cilantro
- Salt and pepper, to taste

Preparation:

1. Preheat the oven to 400°F (204°C).

2. In a small bowl, mix the orange juice, lemon juice, lime juice, and cilantro.

3. Place the tilapia filet on a piece of parchment paper and drizzle with olive oil.

4. Pour the citrus mixture on top of the tilapia filet and pat it to adhere.

5. Place the tilapia filet on a baking sheet and bake in the preheated oven for 10-12 minutes, or until the fish flakes easily with a fork and is opaque in the center. Serve hot.

Nutritional value (approximate): 250 calories, 15g protein, 1g fiber, 10g fat, 8g carbohydrates

Ginger Halibut

Serving: One
Cooking Time: 20 minutes

Ingredients:
• 1/2 lb halibut filet

•1/2 tbsp olive oil

•1/4 cup thinly sliced ginger

•Salt and pepper, to taste

Preparation:

1. Preheat the oven to 400°F (204°C).

2. In a small bowl, mix salt and pepper to taste.

3. Place the halibut filet on a piece of parchment paper and drizzle with olive oil.

4. Arrange the ginger slices on top of the halibut filet and pat them to adhere.

5. Place the halibut filet on a baking sheet and bake in the preheated oven for 10-12 minutes, or until the fish flakes easily with a fork and is opaque in the center. Serve hot.

Nutritional value (approximate): 250 calories, 15g protein, 1g fiber, 10

Tuna Puttanesca

Serving: One

Ingredients:

•1/2 cup whole wheat spaghetti

•1/2 tbsp olive oil

•1/4 onion, chopped

•1 garlic clove, minced

•1/2 can (14.5 oz) diced tomatoes

•1/4 tsp red pepper flakes

•1/4 tsp dried oregano

•1/4 cup pitted kalamata olives, chopped

•1/4 can (2 oz) anchovy fillets, drained and chopped

•1/2 can (5 oz) tuna, drained

•Salt and pepper to taste

Preparation:

1. Cook spaghetti according to package instructions.
2. In a pan, heat olive oil over medium heat.

3. Add onion and garlic and sauté until tender.

4. Add diced tomatoes, red pepper flakes, and oregano. Simmer for 5 minutes.

5. Add olives, anchovy fillets, and tuna. Cook for 2-3 minutes. Serve over cooked spaghetti.

Nutritional Value: Calories: 450, Fat: 16g Carbohydrates: 47g, Fiber: 9g, Protein: 32g

Miso Glazed Black Cod

Serving: One

Ingredients:
- 1 black cod filet (6 oz)
- 1 tbsp sake
- 1 tbsp mirin
- 1 tbsp white miso paste
- 1 tsp sugar

Preparation:

1. Preheat the oven to 400°F.

2. In a small saucepan, combine sake and mirin. Bring to a boil and let simmer for 1-2 minutes to evaporate the alcohol.

3. Add miso paste and sugar. Stir until smooth. Place black cod fillet on a baking sheet lined with parchment paper.

4. Brush miso glaze on top of the filet.

5. Bake for 10-12 minutes or until the fish is cooked through.

Nutritional Value: Calories: 200,Fat: 6g Carbohydrates: 7g, Fiber: 0g, Protein: 28g

Shrimp and Spinach Spaghetti

Serving: One

Ingredients:
- 1/2 cup whole wheat spaghetti
- 1/2 tbsp olive oil
- 1 garlic clove, minced
- 1/2 cup cherry tomatoes, halved
- 1/2 cup baby spinach
- 1/4 lb shrimp, peeled and deveined
- Salt and pepper to taste

Preparation:

1. Cook spaghetti according to package instructions.

2. In a pan, heat olive oil over medium heat.

3. Add garlic and sauté until fragrant.

4. Add cherry tomatoes and cook until they start to soften.

5. Add baby spinach and cook until wilted.

6. Add shrimp and cook until pink. Serve over cooked spaghetti.

Nutritional Value: Calories: 300,Fat: 8g
Carbohydrates: 35g, Fiber: 7g, Protein: 22g

CHAPTER EIGHT

Salad Recipes

Breakfast Salad

Serving: One

Cooking Time: 10 minutes

Ingredients:

•½ cup mixed greens (baby spinach, arugula, kale)

•¼ cup sliced or diced avocado

•2 scrambled eggs (cooked with 1 tsp olive oil)

•20 berries (mixed berries or blueberries)

•¼ cup chopped walnuts

•1-2 tbsp balsamic vinaigrette dressing (oil-based with vinegar)

Preparation:

1. Toss together greens, avocado, eggs, berries, and walnuts in a bowl.

2. Drizzle with balsamic vinaigrette and enjoy!

Nutritional Value: Calories: 350,Protein: 15g
Fat: 20g, Carbohydrates: 25g, Fiber: 5g

Brain Healthy Salad

Serving: One
Cooking Time: 15 minutes

Ingredients:
•½ cup quinoa (cooked)
•¼ cup chopped bell peppers (red and yellow)
•¼ cup chopped broccoli florets

•¼ cup chopped red onion

•20 blueberries

•1 tbsp pumpkin seeds

•2 tbsp lemon vinaigrette dressing (oil-based with vinegar)

Preparation:

1. Cook quinoa according to package instructions.

2. Steam or lightly sauté broccoli florets until tender.

3. Combine quinoa, bell peppers, broccoli, onion, blueberries, and pumpkin seeds in a bowl.

4. Drizzle with lemon vinaigrette and toss to coat.

Nutritional Value: Calories: 300,Protein: 8g

Fat: 12g, Carbohydrates: 40g, Fiber: 6g

Caprese Salad Skewers

Serving: One

Cooking Time: 5 minutes

Ingredients:

•5 cherry tomatoes

•5 small mozzarella balls (bocconcini)

•5 fresh basil leaves

•Drizzle of olive oil

•Balsamic reduction (optional)

Preparation:

1. Thread cherry tomato, mozzarella ball, and basil leaf onto a skewer. Repeat for 5 skewers.

2. Drizzle with olive oil and balsamic reduction (if using).

Nutritional Value: Calories: 200,Protein: 10g

Fat: 10g, Carbohydrates: 10g, Fiber: 1g

Superfood Quinoa Salad

Serving: One

Cooking Time: 15 minutes

Ingredients:

•½ cup cooked quinoa

•¼ cup roasted sweet potato cubes

•¼ cup diced avocado

•½ cup black beans (rinsed and drained)

•½ cup chopped kale

•1 tbsp chopped cilantro

•2 tbsp lime vinaigrette dressing (oil-based with vinegar)

Preparation:

1. Roast sweet potato cubes until tender.

2. Combine quinoa, sweet potato, avocado, black beans, kale, and cilantro in a bowl.

3. Drizzle with lime vinaigrette and toss to coat.

Nutritional Value: Calories: 400,Protein: 15g
Fat: 15g, Carbohydrates: 50g, Fiber: 8g

Asian-Inspired Sesame Ginger Salad

Serving: One
Cooking Time: 10 minutes

Ingredients:
•2 cups mixed greens (baby spinach, romaine)

•½ cup shredded chicken breast (grilled or rotisserie)

•¼ cup sliced cucumber

•¼ cup shredded carrots

•2 tbsp cooked edamame

•1 tbsp chopped scallions

•1 tsp sesame seeds

•1 tbsp sesame ginger dressing (oil-based, low-sugar)

Preparation:

1. In a bowl, combine greens, chicken, cucumber, carrots, edamame, and scallions.

2. Drizzle with sesame ginger dressing and sprinkle with sesame seeds.

3. Toss to coat and enjoy!

Nutritional Value: Calories: 300,Protein: 20g

Fat: 10g, Carbohydrates: 15g, Fiber: 2g

Tabbouleh Salad

Serving: One

Cooking Time: 20 minutes

Ingredients:

•½ cup bulgur (cooked)

•1 cup chopped tomatoes

•1/2 cup chopped parsley

•1/4 cup chopped mint

•2 tbsp chopped cucumber

•1 tbsp lemon juice

•1 tbsp olive oil

Preparation:

1. Cook bulgur according to package instructions.

2. Combine bulgur, tomatoes, parsley, mint, and cucumber in a bowl.

3. Whisk together lemon juice and olive oil, then drizzle over the salad.

4. Toss to coat and chill for at least 30 minutes before serving.

Nutritional Value: Calories: 250,Protein: 5g Fat: 5g, Carbohydrates: 40g, Fiber: 5g

Mediterranean Chickpea Salad

Serving: One

Cooking Time: 15 minutes

Ingredients:

•½ cup cooked chickpeas

•¼ cup chopped cucumber

•¼ cup chopped tomatoes

•¼ cup chopped red onion

- 1 tbsp chopped olives
- 1 tbsp crumbled feta cheese
- 1 tbsp olive oil
- 1 tsp lemon juice
- Herbs of choice (oregano, thyme, parsley)

Preparation:

1. Combine chickpeas, cucumber, tomatoes, onion, olives, and feta cheese in a bowl.

2. Whisk together olive oil, lemon juice, and herbs, then drizzle over the salad.

3. Toss to coat and enjoy!

Nutritional Value: Calories: 300,Protein: 10g

Fat: 10g, Carbohydrates: 30g, Fiber: 5g

Classic Greek Salad

Serving: One
Cooking Time: 10 minutes

Ingredients:

- 2 cups mixed greens (baby spinach, romaine)
- ½ cup diced tomatoes
- ½ cup chopped cucumber
- ¼ cup crumbled feta cheese
- 2 Kalamata olives (sliced)
- 1 tbsp red onion (diced)
- 1 tsp dried oregano
- 1 tbsp olive oil
- 1 tbsp lemon juice

Preparation:

1. Combine greens, tomatoes, cucumber, feta cheese, olives, and onion in a bowl.

2. Sprinkle with oregano.

3. Whisk together olive oil and lemon juice, then drizzle over the salad.

4. Toss to coat and enjoy!

Nutritional Value: Calories: 250,Protein: 8g Fat: 10g, Carbohydrates: 15g, Fiber: 2g

CHAPTER NINE

Snack Recipes

Fried Mushrooms

Serving: One

Cooking Time: 15 minutes

Ingredients:

•4-5 portobello mushrooms (sliced)

•1 tbsp olive oil

•1/4 tsp dried thyme

•Salt and pepper to taste

Preparation:

1. Preheat the oven to 400°F (200°C).

2. Toss mushrooms with olive oil, thyme, salt, and pepper.

3. Spread on a baking sheet and bake for 15 minutes, flipping halfway through.

4. Enjoy as is or with a small dollop of Greek yogurt (optional).

Nutritional Value: Calories: 150,Protein: 4g Fat: 5g, Carbohydrates: 15g, Fiber: 2g

Zucchini Dip

Serving: One
Cooking Time: 20 minutes

Ingredients:
- 1 small zucchini (spiralized)
- 1/4 cup hummus
- 1 tbsp Greek yogurt
- 1 tsp lemon juice
- 1/4 tsp garlic powder
- Fresh herbs of choice (parsley, dill)

Preparation:

1. Spiralize zucchini or cut into thin strips.

2. Toss with lemon juice and set aside for 5 minutes.

3. Combine hummus, Greek yogurt, garlic powder, and herbs in a blender or food processor.

4. Pulse until smooth. Serve zucchini noodles with hummus dip and enjoy!

Nutritional Value: Calories: 200, Protein: 8g
Fat: 5g, Carbohydrates: 30g, Fiber: 5g

Cauliflower Popcorn

Serving: One
Cooking Time: 20 minutes

Ingredients:

•1 cup cauliflower florets

•1 tbsp olive oil

•1/4 tsp paprika

•1/4 tsp garlic powder

•Salt and pepper to taste

Preparation:

1. Preheat the oven to 400°F (200°C).

2. Toss cauliflower with olive oil, paprika, garlic powder, salt, and pepper.

3. Spread on a baking sheet and bake for 20 minutes, tossing occasionally, until crispy.

Nutritional Value: Calories: 100,Protein: 2g Fat: 4g, Carbohydrates: 15g, Fiber: 2g

Almond Butter Stuffed Dates

Serving: 2-3 dates

Cooking Time: 5 minutes

Ingredients:

•2-3 Medjool dates (pitted)

•1 tbsp almond butter

•Chopped nuts or seeds (optional)

Preparation:

1. Stuff each date with 1-2 teaspoons of almond butter.

2. Sprinkle with chopped nuts or seeds (optional).

3. Enjoy a sweet and satisfying snack!

Nutritional Value per Date: Calories: 50
Protein: 1g, Fat: 2g, Carbohydrates: 10g,
Fiber: 1g

Rainbow Fruit Salad

Serving: 1
Cooking Time: 5 minutes

Ingredients:

•1/4 cup blueberries

•1/4 cup strawberries

•1/4 cup pineapple chunks

•1/4 cup green grapes

•1/4 cup orange slices

•1 tbsp Greek yogurt (optional)

Preparation:

1. Combine all fruits in a bowl.

2. Top with Greek yogurt (optional) and enjoy!

Nutritional Value: Calories: 150,Protein: 1g Fat: 0g, Carbohydrates: 30g, Fiber: 3g

Carrot Cashew Pâté

Serving: 1-2 slices of bread
Cooking Time: 15 minutes

Ingredients:
•1 small carrot (roasted)
•1/4 cup cashews (roasted)
•1 tbsp hummus
•1 tbsp lemon juice
•1/4 tsp cumin
•Salt and pepper to taste

Preparation:

1. Roast the carrot in the oven at 400°F (200°C) for 20-25 minutes until tender.

2. Combine roasted carrots, cashews, hummus, lemon juice, cumin, salt, and pepper in a blender or food processor.

3. Pulse until smooth and creamy.

4. Spread on whole-grain crackers or bread and enjoy!

Nutritional Value: Calories: 200,Protein: 5g Fat: 10g, Carbohydrates: 20g, Fiber: 3g

Snacky Chickpeas

Serving: 1/2 cup
Cooking Time: 20 minutes

Ingredients:
•1/2 cup dried chickpeas (soaked overnight)

•1 tbsp olive oil

•1/4 tsp curry powder

•1/4 tsp smoked paprika

•Salt and pepper to taste

Preparation:

1. Preheat the oven to 400°F (200°C).

2. Drain and rinse soaked chickpeas.

3. Toss chickpeas with olive oil, curry powder, paprika, salt, and pepper.

4. Spread on a baking sheet and bake for 20 minutes, tossing occasionally, until crispy.

Nutritional Value: Calories: 200,Protein: 8g Fat: 5g, Carbohydrates: 30g, Fiber: 5g

Bruschetta

Serving: 1 slice of bread

Cooking Time: 10 minutes

Ingredients:

•1 slice whole-wheat bread

•1/4 cup chopped tomatoes

•1 tbsp chopped red onion

•1 tbsp olive oil

•1/4 tsp balsamic vinegar

•Fresh basil leaves

Preparation:

1. Toast the bread slice.

2. Combine chopped tomatoes, red onion, olive oil, and balsamic vinegar in a bowl.

3. Top the toasted bread with the tomato mixture and garnish with fresh basil leaves.

Nutritional Value: Calories: 150,Protein: 2g Fat: 5g, Carbohydrates: 25g, Fiber: 2g

Edamame with Sea Salt

Serving: 1/2 cup

Cooking Time: 5 minutes

Ingredients:

•1/2 cup frozen edamame (steamed or shelled)
•Pinch of sea salt

Preparation:

1. Steam or microwave the frozen edamame according to package instructions.

2. Sprinkle it with a pinch of sea salt and enjoy!

Nutritional Value: Calories: 100,Protein: 8g

Fat: 2g, Carbohydrates: 10g, Fiber: 4g

CHAPTER TEN

Dessert Recipes

Chickpea Blondies

Serving: One

Cooking Time: 20 minutes

Ingredients:

•1/2 cup mashed chickpeas

•1/4 cup almond flour

•1/4 cup rolled oats

•2 tbsp maple syrup

•1 tbsp nut butter (almond, peanut)

•1/4 tsp baking powder

•1/4 tsp cinnamon

•Pinch of salt

Preparation:

1. Preheat the oven to 350°F (175°C).

2. Combine all ingredients in a bowl and mix well.

3. Spread the mixture into a small baking dish lined with parchment paper.

4. Bake for 20 minutes, or until golden brown and firm.

Nutritional Value: Calories: 250,Protein: 8g Fat: 10g, Carbohydrates: 30g, Fiber: 5g

Homestyle Apple Pie

Serving: 1 individual ramekin
Cooking Time: 30 minutes

Ingredients:
- 1 small apple, sliced
- 1/4 cup rolled oats
- 1 tbsp chopped walnuts
- 1 tsp cinnamon

•1 tsp lemon juice

•1 tsp honey

Preparation:

1. Preheat the oven to 375°F (190°C).

2. Toss apple slices with lemon juice.

3. Combine oats, walnuts, and cinnamon in a small bowl.

4. Layer apple slices in a ramekin, sprinkle with oat mixture and drizzle with honey.

5. Bake for 30 minutes, or until apples are tender and the topping is golden brown.

Nutritional Value: Calories: 200,Protein: 2g Fat: 8g, Carbohydrates: 35g, Fiber: 5g

Cranberry Pear Crisp

Serving: 1 small ramekin
Cooking Time: 30 minutes

Ingredients:

•1/2 cup chopped pears

•1/4 cup chopped cranberries

•1/4 cup rolled oats

•1 tbsp chopped almonds

•1 tsp cinnamon

•1 tsp honey

Preparation:

1. Preheat the oven to 375°F (190°C).

2. Combine pears and cranberries in a ramekin.

3. Mix oats, almonds, cinnamon, and honey in a bowl.

4. Sprinkle topping over fruit and bake for 30 minutes, or until golden brown and bubbly.

Nutritional Value: Calories: 250, Protein: 2g
Fat: 8g, Carbohydrates: 40g, Fiber: 5g

Summer Fruit Pops

Serving: 2-3 pops
Cooking Time: 2 hours + freezing time

Ingredients:
•1 cup mixed berries (blueberries, raspberries, strawberries)
•1/2 banana, mashed
•1/4 cup plain Greek yogurt
•1 tbsp lemon juice
Preparation:

1. Blend berries, banana, yogurt, and lemon juice until smooth.

2. Pour into popsicle molds and freeze for at least 2 hours.

Nutritional Value per Pop: Calories: 60, Protein: 2g, Fat: 1g, Carbohydrates: 15g, Fiber: 1g

Banana Nut Mug Cake

Serving: 1 mug

Cooking Time: 2 minutes

Ingredients:

• 1/4 cup mashed banana

• 2 tbsp rolled oats

• 1 tsp chopped nuts (walnuts, almonds)

• 1 tsp chocolate chips (optional)

• 1 tsp milk

Preparation:

1. Mix all ingredients in a mug.

2. Microwave on high for 2 minutes, or until cooked through.

Nutritional Value: Calories: 150,Protein: 2g Fat: 5g, Carbohydrates: 25g, Fiber: 2g

Blueberry Tahini Crisp

Serving: 1 small ramekin
Cooking Time: 30 minutes

Ingredients:

- 1/2 cup blueberries
- 1/4 cup rolled oats
- 1 tbsp chopped almonds
- 1 tbsp tahini
- 1 tbsp honey
- 1 tsp cinnamon

Preparation:

1. Preheat the oven to 375°F (190°C).

2. Combine blueberries with a squeeze of lemon juice.

3. Mix oats, almonds, tahini, honey, and cinnamon in a bowl.

4. Sprinkle topping over blueberries and bake for 30 minutes, or until golden brown and bubbly.

Nutritional Value: Calories: 280,Protein: 5g Fat: 12g, Carbohydrates: 35g, Fiber: 5g

Greek Yogurt Berry Popsicles

Serving: 2-3 pops

Cooking Time: 2 hours + freezing time

Ingredients:

•1/2 cup plain Greek yogurt

•1/4 cup mixed berries (blueberries, raspberries)

•1 tbsp honey

•1/4 tsp vanilla extract

Preparation:

1. Blend yogurt, berries, honey, and vanilla extract until smooth.

2. Pour into popsicle molds and freeze for at least 2 hours.

Nutritional Value per Pop: Calories: 70, Protein: 4g, Fat: 0g, Carbohydrates: 15g Fiber: 1g

Maple Pecan Granola with Olive Oil

Serving: 1/4 cup

Cooking Time: 20 minutes

Ingredients:

•1/4 cup rolled oats

•1 tbsp chopped pecans

•1 tsp olive oil

•1 tsp maple syrup

•1/4 tsp cinnamon

Preparation:

1. Preheat the oven to 350°F (175°C).

2. Toss oats, pecans, olive oil, maple syrup, and cinnamon in a bowl.

3. Spread on a baking sheet and bake for 20 minutes, or until golden brown and crispy.

4. Enjoy with plain yogurt or fresh fruit for a complete dessert.

Nutritional Value per Serving: Calories: 150

Protein: 2g, Fat: 8g, Carbohydrates: 20g

7-DAY MEAL PLAN

Day 1

Breakfast: Nutty Oatmeal

Lunch: Greek Chicken Pita Pocket

Dinner: Cumin Salmon

Snack: Rainbow fruit salad

Day 2

Breakfast: Banana Cookies

Lunch: Brussels Sprout Chicken Tacos

Dinner: Vegetable Succotash

Snack: Stuffed Dates with Almond Butter

Day 3

Breakfast: Strawberry Yoghurt

Lunch: Spicy Citrus Shrimp

Dinner: Pesto Zoodles with Cherry Tomatoes

Snack: Snacky Chickpeas

Day 4

Breakfast: Whole Grain Breakfast Porridge

Lunch: Mediterranean Tuna Salad

Dinner: Chicken Couscous

Snack: Fried Mushrooms

Day 5

Breakfast: Chickpea Cookie Dough

Lunch: Portobello Sandwiches

Dinner: Cashew Turkey Medley

Snack: Zucchini Dip

Day 6

Breakfast: Berry Bliss Smoothie

Lunch: Chili Collard Greens

Dinner: Walnut-Crusted Baked Cod

Snack: Cauliflower Popcorn

Day 7

Breakfast: Quinoa Porridge
Lunch: Colorful Gumbo
Dinner: Baked Mackerel
Snack: Edamame with Sea Salt

Feel free to adjust the plan based on your preferences and dietary needs. Enjoy your delicious and nutritious meals!

CONCLUSION

In concluding the "Mind Diet Cookbook For One," we embark on a journey that transcends mere culinary exploration, reaching into the realm of cognitive empowerment and holistic well-being. Through a meticulously crafted collection of breakfast delights, luscious lunch ideas, dinner delights, savory soups and stews, fantastic fish and seafood dishes, sumptuous salads, tempting snacks, and divine desserts, this cookbook has laid the foundation for a lifestyle centered around mindful eating and brain health. The recipes provided are not merely a list of ingredients and instructions but a testament to the potential transformative power that lies within our daily food choices.

As we savor the Nutty Oatmeal, relish the Greek Chicken Pita Pocket, and indulge in the Chicky Blondies, we are nurturing not just our bodies but our minds. The Mind Diet principles integrated into each recipe offer a roadmap for reducing the risk of neurodegenerative disorders and promoting cognitive vitality. To fully embrace this culinary voyage, remember that adaptation is key. Tailor the Mind Diet to your individual needs, preferences, and cultural influences. Whether you're savoring the simplicity of a breakfast croissant or diving into the richness of a colorful gumbo, let each meal be a celebration of your commitment to both physical and mental well-being.

In making the Mind Diet a cornerstone of your daily life, you're not just embracing a cookbook; you're adopting a lifestyle that honors your body and mind.

It's not just about what you eat; it's about the nourishment you provide to the intricate workings of your brain. So, dear reader, let each recipe be a step towards a healthier, more vibrant you. The power to cultivate a resilient mind lies within your kitchen – a journey worth savoring, one mindful meal at a time.